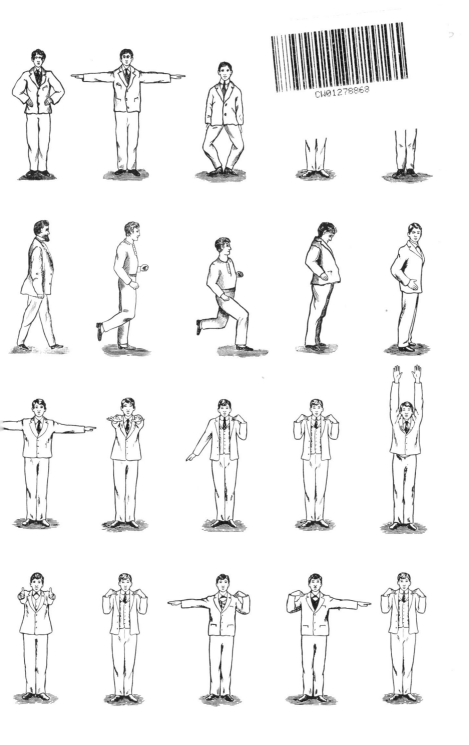

CW01278868

A FITNESS JOURNAL

for

Gentlemen

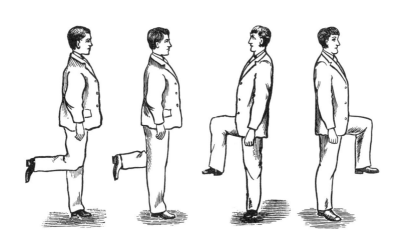

PERSONAL DETAILS

Title/rank ....

Surname ....

Forename ....

Address ....

....

....

....

E-mail ....

Home telephone ....

Mobile telephone ....

Office telephone ....

USEFUL NUMBERS

Accountant's telephone ....

Bank's telephone ....

Stockbroker's telephone ....

Tailor's telephone ....

A GENTLEMAN'S MEASUREMENT GUIDE

1. Collar ....

2. Chest ....

3. Waist ....

4. Sleeve ....

5. Inside leg ....

FOUR-WEEK FITNESS PLANNER

WEEK 1

	EXERCISE(S)	REPETITIONS	RESTING HEART RATE	FINAL HEART RATE
Monday				
Tuesday				
Wednesday				
Thursday				
Friday				
Saturday				
Sunday				

WEEK 2

	EXERCISE(S)	REPETITIONS	RESTING HEART RATE	FINAL HEART RATE
Monday				
Tuesday				
Wednesday				
Thursday				
Friday				
Saturday				
Sunday				

WEEK 3

	EXERCISE(S)	REPETITIONS	RESTING HEART RATE	FINAL HEART RATE
Monday				
Tuesday				
Wednesday				
Thursday				
Friday				
Saturday				
Sunday				

WEEK 4

	EXERCISE(S)	REPETITIONS	RESTING HEART RATE	FINAL HEART RATE
Monday				
Tuesday				
Wednesday				
Thursday				
Friday				
Saturday				
Sunday				

Toe-standing I   *Toe-standing II*

Certainly the man who is blessed with firm, elastic muscles,
*an erect carriage and a state of general **physical fitness***
possesses a formidable equipment for the battle of life.

To cure the mind's wrong bias, spleen,
Some recommend the bowling green,
Some, hilly walks; all, **exercise**

– MATHEW GREEN, 'THE SPLEEN' (1737)

*The proper standing position for man gives **freedom of action** to the lungs and all the other organs of the body. At first the position will be tiring, if one is not accustomed to standing erect, and considerable practice may be necessary in order to make it a natural habit.*

Correct standing

Close standing

Heave-standing

*Exercise in moderation and the symmetrical development of the body are of the greatest value in maintaining a state of health and **vital efficiency**.*

Heave-standing   *Wing-standing*   *Yard-standing*

Knee-bend-standing

Bend-standing

Rest-standing

*When **health** is absent,*
wisdom can not reveal itself,
art can not become manifest,
strength can not be exerted,
wealth is useless,
and reason is powerless.

– HEROPHILOS (300 BCE)

Sitting so that the spine is arched forwards is a
pernicious habit _that interferes with proper respiration._

Correct sitting   _Incorrect sitting_

When taking breathing exercises,
do them with a will and **heartily***,*
fixing the attention on the lungs
and the muscles of respiration.

To **breathe properly**, there must be free action of the chest and abdominal muscles. During inspiration there should be an increase in the three diameters of the chest: antero-posterior, lateral and vertical.

Deep Breathing
with Perscussion

Deep Breathing,
sounding Ah!

Explosive Breathing

*Better to hunt in fields, for **health** unbought,*
Than fee the doctor for a nauseous draught.
*The wise, for cure, on **exercise** depend;*
God never made his work, for man to mend.

– JOHN DRYDEN, *'TO MY HONOURED KINSMAN JOHN DRIDEN'* (1700)

Walk up stairs as you would on the level, and you will be able to accomplish with **comparative ease** *what is usually considered to be a wearisome task.*

Incorrect Position for Climbing Stairs

Correct Position for Climbing Stairs

Exercise stimulates the circulation, sending the
purified blood *bounding through the arteries and into*
the minute capillaries throughout the entire body.

Walking is sometimes described as an intermittent falling forwards, with a foot thrust forwards just in time to **prevent falling**.

Walking

Incorrect Position for Running

Correct Position for Running

*A graceful carriage, which is one of the primary elements of beauty, may be cultivated by practising the **light gymnastics** in this journal.*

*Combined with the correct standing position, bending and twisting the head will be ample to ensure the **health** and **mobility** of the upper spine and neck.*

Wing-Standing,
Head-Bending

Wing-Standing,
Head-Twisting I

Wing-Standing,
Head-Twisting II

*By constant **exercise** one develops freedom of movement – for virtuous deeds.*

– DIOGENES (4TH CENTURY BCE)

*Movements of the trunk should be taken rather slowly and deliberately as a rule. In this way the **greatest benefit** will be derived.*

Wing-Standing, Trunk-Bending, Forwards

Wing-Standing, Trunk-Bending, Backwards

Wing-Standing, Trunk-Bending, Sidewards

Wing-Standing, Trunk-Twisting

*Daily **exercise** out-of-doors is a wonderful beautifier.*
It improves the circulation, gives tone to the nerves, rounds out
the muscles and imparts stay and stamina to the system.

Arm-Raising, Forwards   *Arm-Raising, Outwards*   *Standing, Arm-Raising,
Backwards*

*For persons in reasonably **vigorous health** it is coming to be considered that linen mesh garments afford the ideal material to put next to the skin. Such fabrics, while they do not have the cold clammy feel of closely-woven linen, receive and throw off quickly all moisture from the body, thus keeping the skin dry and clean.*

Standing,
Arm-Stretching

Standing, Arm-
Stretching, Outwards

Standing, Arm-
Stretching, Forwards

Standing, Arm-
Stretching, Upwards

*The flowering of civilization is the
finished man, the man of sense,
of grace, of accomplishment,
of social power – **the gentleman.***

– EMERSON, 'FORTUNE OF THE REPUBLIC' (1878)

Brisk walking, with chest well expanded,
shoulders back and arms hanging naturally
at the sides, is the best all-round **exercise**.

Bend-Standing, Arm-Extending, Downwards I

Bend-Standing, Arm-Extending, Downwards II

Bend-Standing, Arm-Extending, Downwards III

Bend-Standing, Arm-Extending, Downwards IV

*Deep breathing, practised night and morning, **will do wonders** in the way of broadening and deepening the chest, and filling up the unsightly hollows of the neck and chest.*

*Look to your health; and if you have it, praise God, and value it next to a good conscience; for health is the second blessing that we mortals are capable of; **a blessing** that money cannot buy.*

– IZAAK WALTON, 'THE COMPLEAT ANGLER' (1653)

*This **exercise** should be taken with deliberation.
An effort should be made to reach as far as possible
with the fingers while executing the movement.*

*Bend-Standing, Arm-
Extending, Forwards I*

*Bend-Standing, Arm-
Extending, Forwards II*

*Bend-Standing, Arm-
Extending, Forwards III*

*Bend-Standing, Arm-
Extending, Forwards IV*

The preservation of health is a duty.
Few seem conscious that there is such
*a thing as **physical morality.***

HERBERT SPENCER, *'EDUCATION'* (1861)

*Bend-Standing, Arm-
Extending, Outwards I*

*Bend-Standing, Arm-
Extending, Outwards II*

*Bend-Standing, Arm-
Extending, Outwards III*

*Bend-Standing, Arm-
Extending, Outwards IV*

Bend-Standing, Arm-Extending, Upwards I

Bend-Standing, Arm-Extending, Upwards II

Bend-Standing, Arm-Extending, Upwards III

Bend-Standing, Arm-Extending, Upwards IV

*Sleep on a hard bed. Follow a **wholesome diet**, eating largely dry, hard foods. Avoid cheap novels and exciting stories.*

Throughout these different positions, the arms should always be kept **well extended**, and at the same height as the shoulders.

Heave-Standing,
Arm-Extending

Heave-Standing,
Fore-Arm Rotating, Forwards

Standing,
Swimming

*A good condition of muscular fitness usually brings sound, **refreshing sleep**, and a well-balanced nervous system.*

Standing, Arm-Twisting
& Arm Rotating I

Standing, Arm-Twisting
& Arm Rotating II

Standing, Arm-Twisting
& Arm Rotating II

Whether sitting, walking, climbing or running, one should aim to maintain a correct, upright posture, which will ensure both **elegance** *and* **symmetry**.

*This is an excellent **exercise** to develop the chest
and increase the breathing capacity.*

*Standing, Arms-Flinging,
Backwards I*

*Standing, Arms-Flinging,
Backwards II*

*The **sovereign invigorator**
of the body is exercise,
and of all the exercises,
walking is best.*

– THOMAS JEFFERSON (1786)

*Whatever is injurious to the **health** of the body must also spoil its beauty; and, on the other hand, that which makes for **health** and **long life**, likewise must make for beauty.*

*Standing, Fingers-Bending
& Extending I*

*Standing, Fingers-Bending
& Extending II*

*Standing, Fingers-Bending
& Extending III*

*Exercise contributes to that **calm self-possession**, that well-balanced air, that combination of strength and gentleness, which is so attractive in either sex.*

Wing-Standing,
Leg-Extending, Sidewards I

Wing-Standing,
Leg-Extending, Sidewards II

*Flabby muscles may be taken to denote a general mental, if not moral, flabbiness; while the training of the muscles, kept within the proper limits, **wonderfully enlivens the spirits** and the general tone of a person.*

*The development of a **supple** and **strong physique**
brings with it the resultant benefits of improved posture
and greater overall physical well-being.*

Standing, Leg-Extending,
Forwards (Left Leg)

Standing, Leg-Extending,
Forwards (Right Leg)

Riding, cycling, tennis, croquet
and golf are all very good
taken in moderation.

*This position is one of erectness, dignity and grace, and pleasing to behold. More, it gives **spring** and **elasticity** to the step, and in walking minimises jarring of the spine.*

Standing, Leg-Extending, Backwards (Right Leg)

Standing, Leg-Extending, Backwards (Right Leg)

Standing, Leg-Extending, Backwards (Left Leg)

Standing, Leg-Extending, Backwards (Left Leg)

*Rosy-complexion'd **Health** thy steps attends,*
And exercise thy lasting youth defends.

– JOHN GAY, *'TRIVIA'* (1716)

Wing-Standing,
Leg-Twisting I

Wing-Standing,
Leg-Twisting II

Wing-Standing,
Leg-Twisting III

Wing-Standing,
Leg-Twisting IV

Wing-Standing,
Leg-Twisting V

Wing-Standing,
Leg-Twisting VI

*Many of these movements require **careful balancing** and hence must be taken very accurately. There is always a tendency to neglect the position of the trunk in doing leg movements, but this is a mistake. The trunk should be kept erect, as described in the correct standing position.*

*Exercise in moderation and the symmetrical development of the body are of the greatest value in maintaining a state of health and **vital efficiency**.*

Standing,
Leg-Lifting I

Standing,
Leg-Lifting II

Standing,
Leg-Bending I

Standing,
Leg-Bending II

Exercise greatly aids digestion, thus improving the nutrition of all organs, including the brain.

If one guiding principle be sought for upon which
*life can be remodelled, we commend the "**Simple Life**."*
Turn one's back on the soul-deadening artificialities and
machine methods, and the mad, feverish rush after wealth
which are eating into the very heart of present-day society.

Wing-Standing,
Knee-Bending I

Wing-Standing,
Knee-Bending II

Wing-Standing,
Knee-Bending III

*Sufficient use of the muscles to keep them in **good condition** is favourable to the accomplishment of the best mental work.*

Wing-Standing,
Heel-Raising I

Wing-Standing,
Heel-Raising II

Exercise quickens breathing,
both in the lungs and in the tissues.

Exercise and *temperance* can
preserve something of our early
strength even in old age.

– CICERO, *'DE SENECTUTE'* (44 BCE)

Standing, Arms-Stretching
with Heel-Raising I

Standing, Arms-Stretching
with Heel-Raising II

Standing, Arms-Stretching
with Heel-Raising III

Standing, Arms-Stretching
with Heel-Raising IV

*When taking arm exercises, let your **mind power** be concentrated on your arms – not painfully, but cheerfully and earnestly.*

Close-Standing,
Arm-Raising, Forwards

Close-Standing,
Arm-Raising, Outwards

Close-Standing,
Arm-Raising, Backwards

There can be no true
*beauty without **health**.*

*Wing-Close-Standing,
Heel-Raising I*

*Wing-Close-Standing,
Heel-Raising II*

Working in the garden is an excellent way
*to **exercise** provided care is taken to avoid an undue*
amount of stooping, which contracts the chest.

Bend-Close-Standing, Arm-Extending, Downwards I

Bend-Close-Standing, Arm-Extending, Downwards II

Bend-Close-Standing, Arm-Extending, Downwards III

Bend-Close-Standing, Arm-Extending, Downwards IV

*Those who think they have not time for bodily **exercise** will sooner or later have to find time for illness.*

– EDWARD STANLEY, 3RD EARL OF DERBY (1873)

Wing-Toe Close-Standing,
Knee Bending I

Wing-Toe Close-Standing,
Knee Bending II

Wing-Toe Close-Standing,
Knee Bending III

*Swimming is a capital exercise for those who wish to acquire a degree of ease and **grace of movement**.*

Wing-Sitting,
Knees-Opening & Closing I

Wing-Sitting,
Knees-Opening & Closing II

*Study the lives of the men who have **left their mark**
in the history of the world, and, though they may differ
in many respects, you will find that they were mostly alike
in possessing a certain firmness of muscular texture, and
the ability to endure severe strain, physical and mental.*

*This exercise is **quite vigorous** and proper care should be taken to avoid strain or over-exertion.*

Wing-Toe-Standing,
Jumping I

Wing-Toe-Standing,
Jumping II

Wing-Toe-Standing,
Jumping III

Wing-Toe-Standing,
Jumping IV

An excellent means of improving the tone of the skin
is the air bath. Disrobe completely, and give the whole body
a vigorous rubbing with a flesh brush or with the bare hand.
Light gymnastics *may also be taken during the air bath.*

Wing-Toe-Standing,
Jumping, Sidewards I

Wing-Toe-Standing,
Jumping, Sidewards II

*Without **health**, life is not life; life is useless.*

– ARIPHON THE SICYONIAN (4TH CENTURY BCE)

Wing-Toe-Standing,
Jumping, Backwards I

Wing-Toe-Standing,
Jumping, Backwards II

Wing-Toe-Standing,
Jumping, Forwards I

Wing-Toe-Standing,
Jumping, Forwards II

First published in the UK in 2010 by
Ivy Press
210 High Street
Lewes
East Sussex BN7 2NS
United Kingdom
www.ivypress.co.uk

This book is not intended as a substitute for the advice of a healthcare professional. If you have any reason to believe you have a condition that affects your health, you must seek professional advice. Consult a qualified healthcare professional before starting.

British Library Cataloguing-in-Publication Data: a catalogue record for this book is available from the British Library.

ISBN: 978-1-907332-16-6

This book was conceived, designed and produced by **Ivy Press**

Printed in China

10 9 8 7 6 5 4 3 2 1

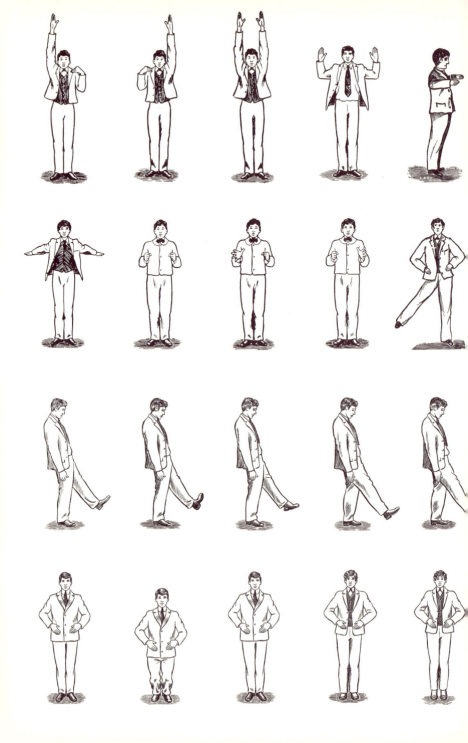